Awareness
in
Prayer

Ethan Penner

For permission requests, write to the publisher, addressed "Attention: Permissions Coordinator," carol@markvictorhansenlibrary.com

Quantity sales special discounts are available on quantity purchases by corporations, associations, and others. For details, contact the publisher at carol@markvictorhansenlibrary.com

Orders by U.S. trade bookstores and wholesalers. Email: carol@markvictorhansenlibrary.com

Cover Design and Book Layout - DBree

Manufactured and printed in the United States of America Distributed globally by markvictorhansenlibrary.com

MVHL

New York | Los Angeles | London | Sydney

ISBN: 979-8-88581-191-0 Hardback
ISBN: 979-8-88581-192-7 Paperback
ISBN: 979-8-88581-193-4 eBook
Library of Congress Control Number: 9798885811910

Contents

Dedication

I dedicate this book to my family. To my mother and father who taught me and guided me and instilled in me a hunger to learn. To my grandparents whose lives were lived in sacrifice, dedicated solely to creating a better future for their children and grandchildren and who set the table for the wonderful lives we've enjoyed. To my amazing wife Marisol, whose passion, love of nature, and incredible maternal instincts are the rock of our family. And to my children, Michael Angel, Daniel, Rebecca, Julianna, and Everest Gobena, may God bless you with a beautiful life filled with learning, joy, service and fulfillment.

Introduction

The Value Proposition

We're not praying to God. We pray to improve
ourselves. God is already perfect.

This book is about using prayer to heighten
awareness and with that awareness to extract
more joy and fulfillment from daily life.
Together, with the benefits of prayer, I believe that
we can create a truly beautiful and purposeful world.

I have been familiar with the prayers in this
book for my whole life. Yet, it wasn't until I had a
miraculous "born again" moment that I began to
focus on the meanings of the words. The resulting
awareness that has come from daily recitation of these
prayers in a state of attentiveness to their meaning
has alerted me to God's presence in all aspects of
the world. And this awareness of the world's divine
perfection has provided me with newfound purpose
and confidence, the foundations of a life of joy
and fulfillment. Even if you have no religion nor a
belief in God, I predict that by following this book's
prayer ritual on a daily basis you too will discover
the Divine perfection of the world and, seeing that

perfection instead of chaos and randomness, you will gain newfound confidence and purpose.

In truth, I am a logician and not really a man of faith. To believe, I must find logic. As I see it, in a world without God lives are reduced to seeking comfort, security, and joy and avoiding pain and discomfort. A world that prioritizes these goals logically must be a world replete with greed and hoarding, laziness and victimhood, envy and crime, and much hate and judgment. In a secular world where the true north is comfort, a society's construct along with its laws and their enforcement only make sense if they produce that for most. When too many feel that they are not getting their fair share of these deliverables, it would be only be natural for them to rebel, both against the authority and the laws that have failed them. Their regard for the law will be akin to the natural inclination to ignore a 30 MPH speed limit on an empty rural road at 2AM. It is logical that in the moments when too many are not comfortable or, in a sense of victimhood feel that they are getting a raw deal, which happens with predictable cyclicality, that we see people ignoring law, turning on each other, and turning the world to horror.

In direct contrast to this secular construct, which is doomed to cyclical failure and much needless suffering, stands the potential for a truly religious world with a deep awareness of God and of God's laws and guidelines that paves the road for living fruitful and meaningful lives. In this world, life is all about learning lessons through an active and aware life that produces growth, as opposed to the pursuit of joy, comfort, and security. Of course, these three things are still desirable and appreciated. But in God's world, created with intelligent design, it is natural to see failure, disappointment, pain, and suffering as purposeful. They represent teaching moments, and thus are not only tolerated but even welcomed. As such, in God's world fear would be illogical, thus we would live with an abundance mentality that leads to true love. In God's world people would actively seek growth, leading to often choosing the harder road rather the easy one. In God's world respect for individual liberty would be natural, as there would be an understanding that every human being is on their own personal and purposeful journey, with unique experiences tailored for that specific individual. In God's world the amassing of material things beyond some level would be undesirable, viewed as a form of gluttony. In such a world, envy would be impossible.

In God's world laws would be respected and viewed as necessary guideposts in the journey of learning and growth. People would not need to be policed, just reminded of their own divine connection. This world is thus far less likely to devolve into revolt, crime, or hatred. It is a world that would not naturally have a homeless or an impoverished class. God's world would be characterized by a sense of personal responsibility, of owning your life rather than blaming others or bad luck, for without this sense there could be no foundation of personal growth. There could be no victimhood in this world, with all realizing they are blessed to have been created by God for a specific purpose.

Jewish Prayer— Is it for me?

The history of Jewish prayer in some form goes back to the existence of the first ancient Jewish temple in Jerusalem, 1000 BCE (or BC), when people brought their animal sacrifices to God and recited some biblical liturgy as well as some other extra-biblical prayers in conjunction with the sacrifices. After the destruction of the second Jewish temple, around 70 CE (or AD), the practice of animal sacrifices ended and gave way to a more robust prayer practice. The foundation of that practice then is identical to today's —with the central two prayers being the "Sh'ma" as well as the Sh'mona Esrai." Obviously, my prayer practice includes these two beautiful and valuable prayers.

Non-Jewish readers might ask why this book and the Jewish-based prayer practice is valuable to them. I have a few different responses to this. First, for Christians, Jesus and all of his apostles were practicing Jews until their death. They lived fully Jewish lives and thus there is a naturally very deep connection between Jews, Jewish life, and Jewish prayer and every single true Christian. I have long believed that the chasm between Christians and Jews is one of the serious problems in our world and have longed for these two practices, born from the same womb, to be reunited in some form under God's laws. It is my hope that through a shared prayer practice, a foundation can be laid for such a reunion.

For non-Christians I say that if you read this book and find value in this prayer ritual, then by all means it is for you. People cannot be coerced to embrace valueless ideas and untruths. Give this book and the prayers a chance, and if it speaks to you, which I believe it will, then embrace it and make it your own. There need not be a name associated with it. God made us all. There is one team—God's creatures—and we're all on it.

1.

The Opener—Thanks!

I offer thanks before You, living and eternal King, for You have mercifully restored my soul within me; Your faithfulness is great.

With these first words and thoughts of the morning I gain an appropriate level of humility which can only help me throughout my upcoming day. I proclaim my dependence upon something far greater than me for my life and I acknowledge, and thus become aware that there is mystery to my existence, and that I am not in control of my life or of too much. This state of humility will position me to be a much better listener throughout my day, to consider the perspectives of others, and to learn and grow from the many lessons that await me in my upcoming day's walkabout.

1

With this opening prayer to my day, I thank God for giving me another day in my body, on this earth, with my family. As I recite this prayer, I realize that my days are finite, which realization creates a different sense of urgency to accomplishing what I would like in my limited time on earth. By expressing gratitude for having been given my day, I become aware that with this gift comes responsibility to live this day to the best of my abilities in every way possible.

Finally, I show my appreciation for having been granted this upcoming day. If I can somehow keep that state of appreciation for my day with me throughout the day, I know that I will touch the world better and will elicit from the world so much more than I might if I did not have that sense.

2.

Water

Blessed are You, Lord our God, King of the universe, who has sanctified us with His commandments, and commanded us concerning the washing of the hands.

There is something magical about water. Our bodies are approximately 60% water, so it is not wrong to say that we are water. When I awaken and the water touches my body, I feel truly alive, as though my state of awakening and awareness is immediately enhanced massively. For me, it is thus not a surprise that the ancient Jewish rituals include a mandating that upon awakening one must touch water and recite this associated prayer.

We are living in a time of extreme degradation of our planet's natural resources, and chief among them is water. More than 25% of humans lack access to clean and safe water. Even in the U.S., long considered the country with the best water, it is now commonplace for those with financial means to drink mostly bottled rather than tap water, and to have home filtration systems that ensure that the water they bathe with is also healthy and free of toxins. This prayer serves to underscore the importance of water in our lives and for me is also a loud alarm that tells me to appreciate the earth's natural resources that sustain our lives, and to be a strong advocate for ensuring that humans be good stewards of the earth and those resources. Obviously, it would be wonderful if more people had this level of awareness imposed upon them each morning as they set out in their day.

3.
My Body Works!

Blessed are you, Lord our God, King of the universe, who has formed man in wisdom, and created within him numerous orifices and cavities. It is revealed and known before the Throne of Your Glory that if but one of them were to be blocked, or one of them were to be opened, it would be impossible to exist even for a short while. Blessed are you Lord, who heals all flesh and performs wonders.

This prayer is both said as a part of the morning prayer ritual as well as after each bowel movement or urination throughout the day. It is a tribute to God for having given us bodies that function as miraculously as they do. With all that science and technology has accomplished, the human body is a technology that is still not even understandable by the finest of minds, let alone replicable. My cardiologist friend, whose skill and caring I probably owe my life to for having identified a genetically defective aortic valve, explained to me one day as we watched a sonogram video of my heart performing on his computer that no one knows how the heart works, and that doctors like him, while doing the best they can, are still mostly in the dark. Again, this prayer is at its core one that should lead to both humility and appreciation, the twin sentiments that ensure a great day upcoming.

In 2018, I experienced my most intense physical pain, which unfortunately lasted for more than a month. From nowhere, a massive hemorrhoid emerged. That this happened on a Friday evening meant that I could not even see a doctor until Monday. I did go to urgent care, but the doctor there not being a colorectal specialist exacerbated my pain by manually trying to force the hemorrhoid back inside of me. That next week I had surgery to remove the hemorrhoid, not realizing that perhaps the worst was yet to come. The pain from the surgery inhibited my body's ability to both urinate or to have bowel movements. The pain from being "stopped up" is truly unimaginable, and I wish it on no one.

However, I have long noted that from extreme pain and suffering also comes extreme good, and this case was no different.

Now, whenever I urinate or have a bowel movement, I have a very deep sense of appreciation that would have been entirely impossible had I not suffered as I had. I say this prayer regularly with deep intensity and with a deep sense of appreciation that brings me to a happy state regardless of what else is occurring at that moment.

4.

My Soul is Divine

My God, the soul which you have given within me is pure. You have created it, You have formed it, you have breathed it into me, and You preserved it within me. You will eventually take it from me and restore it within me in time to come. So long as the soul is within me, I offer thanks to You, Lord my God and God of my fathers, Master of all works, Lord of all souls. Blessed are You Lord, who restores souls to dead bodies.

This prayer alerts me that I am very special because of my direct connection to God, and that I can and should rightly expect a great deal from my life. At the same time, the prayer reminds me that I am not in control at all, thus reinforcing my humility. I love this duality wherein I must dance between the pride of being God's creation and at the very same time the helplessness and humility that comes naturally with the understanding that I have no control, or even an understanding of my life journey. It is my daily goal to live with these seemingly contradictory ideas in mind.

As we grow older in life and experience the inevitable disappointments and frustrations, it is natural and understandable for people to downgrade their expectations for themselves. The dreams of youth get shattered as we realize that we will not be star athletes or movie stars. We may not gain the wealth we had aspired to or have the exciting life we dreamed of. We may not have any fame at all. We may not have created the beautiful family that we had planned for. And with these sad realizations, it is natural for us to look in the mirror and see a pathetic figure—a loser. This prayer is a direct refutation of that sentiment. It is there to remind us that we are God's creation, and that God has breathed a divine level of capacity for greatness into each of us. This prayer lifts our spirits, reminding us that despite all of our failures we are capable of greatness that very day and that we should aim high accordingly. It tells us that the journey of failures were just lessons that we needed to learn to position us to be the great, divinely inspired beings that we are meant to be.

This prayer is also a reminder not to take ourselves or this life too seriously, and to not be too concerned with what we may see, with our limited vision and understanding, as systemic inequities. This world is a practice field. It is a place to try things out and see what happens, and to learn and grow from the experiences. There is a "time to come," a next plane of existence beyond this world where we are bound to gain some more clarity and where all the practice done here on earth will pay dividends. In this practice field, we can't really know too much. We see those who suffer, including ourselves, and wonder what was done to deserve that, with the implication being that the suffering is a punishment or a curse. At the same time, we see those living luxurious lives and it is natural to think "Why them?" It is especially perplexing when we see people we might even know as being not lovely people being rewarded with luxurious lives. This prayer, like a few others in my daily prayer ritual, reminds me that everyone dies and moves on, and that our lives are all mysteries. We are all here on earth living a very personalized existence with experiences that are tailor made for only us. This prayer focuses my attention on the unique journey of my soul, and how during my upcoming day I can best honor it as a gift from God and prepare it for the world to come.

5.

Prayer Sequence

There are a few prayers that are grouped and follow a theme. This next prayer is one of those and the individual prayers will be labeled as being part of the same group, though discussed individually.

* * * * *

The World is Perfect!

Blessed are You, Lord our God, King of the universe, who gives the rooster the understanding to distinguish between day and night.

It was not until I began to pray with awareness that I began to see the incredible value of this prayer. For many decades, I'd rush past this seemingly trite or less consequential prayer without giving it too much thought. Then, in a state of inquiry, when I began to seek meaning in prayer, and resulting awareness, I saw newfound importance and value. While uttering these words that acknowledge the miracle of the rooster's natural built-in timing mechanism, my attention is directed to the many other unseen and underappreciated little things that happen every day that indicate to all of us that there is truly a divine intelligent design to every facet of earth. With this understanding I can then extrapolate to conclude that God created this world and everything in it with intent and purpose. And from this understanding I

14

gain a sense of calm that allows me to live my life without the constant fear that naturally accompanies one who sees life as random and thus irrational and scary. By knowing that God has carefully designed even the most seemingly trivial aspects of earth, I know that everything that occurs is good because this is God's world. I know that even my pain and suffering are designed to benefit me, to teach me, and to make me a better man (soul). And, while I treasure each of the prayers in my daily ritual, this little one-line prayer is thus among my special favorites.

* * * * *

We All Have Blind Spots

Blessed are You, Lord our God, King of the universe, who opens the eyes of the blind.

While most of us can see well with our eyes, in reality we are also all so very blind. That is the nature of being human on earth. We don't know how we got here, why we're here, or what or who brought us here. Much of how we choose to live life involves guesswork. It is through the experience of life, and especially doing so in an aware state, that we can gain some clarity and grow past our born state of blindness. When we can experience life with an appreciation for God and with a framework for living a life of purpose in a world that was designed with purpose, we can begin to see truth. We can then begin to live a meaningful and even intelligent life.

Conversely, without this understanding we are doomed to see a randomness that perpetuates our blindness. In Hebrew, this randomness is captured in the phrase "Tohu Va'vohu," which translates loosely to mean "total chaos." The world is indeed very chaotic on the surface, and so many people find themselves asking questions like "How is it that we have such poor national and international leadership?" "Why is there so much violence and hatred?" Lately, I've been observing how selfish and greedy people are, how many people try to take as much as they can from others while offering the least in value in return. These are all symptoms of a world without a strong connection to God, or that higher power. It is the outcome of a world filled with the blind who desperately grab at anything to find momentary pleasure or the illusion of security.

* * * * *

Liberate Me from My Limitations

Blessed are You, Lord our God, King of the universe, who releases the bound.

Without God in our lives, we easily become entrapped, or bound, by earthly enticements. For some this can take the form unhealthy addictions to substances, or to gambling, or technology, or sexual affirmations, or other forms of conquests such as business achievement or the amassment of money and material things. In this prayer, I acknowledge that it is through my relationship with God that I discovered that my life has meaning and value and purpose, all as a natural part of the world that God has created with purpose. It is through this understanding that I am released from the bounds of the traditional traps that lay in wait for each of us daily.

* * * * *

Help Me Be Proud

Blessed are You, Lord our God, King of the universe, who straightens the bowed.

L ife is challenging and humbling. No one goes through life without many disappointments and frustrations. Sometimes these manifest in physical challenges, sometimes emotional, sometimes financial or professional, sometimes in a relationship gone awry or sometimes due to a lack of any meaningful relationships at all. Sometimes our dreams are shattered, and we are completely lost as to what may come next.

For me, this prayer is an acknowledgment that through my relationship with God and the trust that I have placed in Him to have created a purposeful and meaningful journey for me, I can stand tall and unbowed in the face of all the challenges that may come my way. The resulting confidence, stemming from the fact that I have been created by God and that my journey, however challenging and filled with seeming failures, is one that is meant to be and is divinely guided, enables me to keep my head up when things don't go my way. This faith in my destiny, believing fully that I am always being lead in the right path even if it might not be apparent in the moment, enables me to keep calm during storms and to find the next open door even as doors are being closed all around me.

* * * * *

Nurture Me

Blessed are you, Lord our God, King of the universe, who clothes the naked.

In reality, this particular prayer is not among my favorites, yet I do recite it daily as a part of this sequence of prayers. I am not a fan of clothing, seeing that God created man in his purest and naked form and that clothing is something that conceals that pure form. I actually believe that clothing has two important negative qualities. First, it creates a disconnection between our consciousness and our physical form. When we conceal ourselves behind clothing, it is natural to lose a connection to our bodies. I believe that if we didn't have that concealment, we'd all be fitter and healthier, and not be so complacent as our bodies lose form due to poor eating or lack of movement. Second, clothing can be used as a form of status, with those who are richer able to flex their wealth and gain some false esteem, while those who are poorer finding their lower status reinforced through their clothing options.

I recently asked a rabbi friend for his take on this prayer, and he said that the clothing reference is meant to be metaphorical and that through our closeness to God we are "wrapped" or "clothed" in his glory. I suppose this makes sense and is the thought that I have in mind when I recite this prayer. In the end, I recite this prayer in tribute to the scholars who organized this prayer sequence. Perhaps over time, as I continue to recite this prayer daily, I will gain a new understanding of its meaning.

* * * * *

Give Me the Strength to...

Blessed are You, Lord our God, King of the universe, who gives strength to the weary.

As I mentioned earlier, life is hard and filled with challenges for all. At some point in every life, it is hard to find the strength or courage to get out of bed in the morning to face the next day's challenges. Sometimes we're embarrassed by our failures and unsure if the world will give us another chance to be better. Sometimes we just feel as though we've given all that we have to give and it just wasn't enough. It is in these moments that we can either fold the tent and relegate ourselves to a pathetic future of self-pity or find the strength to stand upright and move forward. For me, knowing that I've been created by God with purpose gives me all the strength that I need to move forward. This prayer is a beautiful reminder of that.

* * * * *

A Reminder to Care for Our Planet

Blessed are You, Lord our God, King of the universe, who spreads forth the earth above the waters.

Most of us reside in cities, with paved streets and big buildings. Too many people have lost their connection to and appreciation of nature. That we are now dealing with all sorts of negative consequences of this lost connection should not be too great a surprise. In cities, we cavalierly create massive amounts of trash each day, bag it, and then toss it down some chute in our building, not giving a moment's thought as to where that will end up. Today, our environment is collapsing under the weight of eight billion people living their lives without any regard for, or even awareness of their dependence upon the earth's natural resources. This prayer alerts me every morning that God created this earth with intelligent design, and it is a gift from God that sustains our lives and thus needs to be cared for.

* * * * *

Guide Me

Blessed are You, Lord our God, King of the universe, who directs the steps of man.

How much of life is free choice and how much is destined to be? This is a question to wrestle with throughout one's life. I love the wording of this prayer as it seems to hint at an answer that lies somewhere in between these two opposing answers. The insinuation here is that God directs our steps but doesn't force them. God is there to guide but we must be aware of his influence in order to feel his gentle hand. If we are willful, we can go against God's guiding hand. If we are unaware, then we're likely to go in a different direction some large percentage of the time. Yet, if we can remain aware of God in our lives, if we can see His daily influences in the world, we can feel His hand alongside us and be guided towards our best path.

* * * * *

Provide for Me

Blessed are You, Lord our God, King of the universe, who has made for me all that I need.

This prayer naturally follows the one preceding it. Together, they tell me that with God's guidance and in God's abundance on earth I have no excuses for my failures other than to look inwards at myself. I alone am responsible for all that I fail to accomplish, and it is my shortcomings that will reveal themselves when I fail. And, in these moments of failure and disappointment, taking full credit, I am in a great position to grow past those shortcomings and improve myself to being a better version of myself. I am here on earth to refine myself, to improve. This life that God has created is a perfect school wherein I can bring my best, fail, learn what is missing, and get better.

It is worth noting here that in some prayer books this prayer is misinterpreted from the Hebrew to read "..., who has provided me with my every need." The Hebrew words in the prayer are clearly not the words for "provided me," but are the word for "made for me," and the difference, while subtle, is profound. If I think that God created a world in which all that I will need has been made for me, I am still required to bring a supreme effort in order to bring those things into my life. However, if I believed that God has provided me with all that I need, I can feel very empty, disappointed, lost, and even betrayed were I to wake up in the morning to see that there is insufficient food to feed my family that day, or I don't have all that I desire. The difference is that the correct interpretation calls for action on our part, in partnership with God, while the misinterpretation is a call for dependence and ultimately a sense of victimhood.

* * * * *

Care for Israel

Blessed are You, Lord our God, King of the universe, who girds Israel with might. Blessed are you, Lord our God, King of the universe, who crowns Israel with glory.

These two prayers seem to go together which is why I've coupled them into one. Israel is the physical foundation of the Jewish people. For two thousand years Jews lived in a diaspora—a people with no homeland of their own, guests in foreign lands. During this time, Jews suffered periodic and sometimes continual persecution. In fact, there is no group other than Jews in world history that has survived nearly as long as a people without a homeland of their own. In the wake of the Holocaust in World War II, when Jews faced their most grave existential crisis, and after a near 2,000 year diaspora, the need for a return to Israel and for a homeland of its own became blatantly apparent. Even the British who controlled Israel at that time, along with other world powers in the U.N., none of whom had ever exhibited any great love for Jews, understood this and ratified Israel as a Jewish nation in 1948.

These twin prayers give thanks to God for bolstering and guiding the nation of Israel. As I write this in 2024, Israel is in the midst of a terrible conflict in Gaza with the terrorist group Hamas, an agent of Iran's Islamic Fundamentalist regime, and the duly elected governing organization of Gaza since Israel left it in 2005, some 19 years ago. This conflict has inspired a global movement of anti-Israel sentiment, that looked at carefully is mostly an anti-Jewish sentiment, which is a stark reminder of the need for a strong Jewish homeland. Simply, there is no Jews without Israel and no Israel without Jews. These two prayers help us to understand and to appreciate that.

* * * * *

Keep Me Close

Blessed are You, Lord our God, King of the universe, who has not made me a stranger.

This prayer celebrates my relationship with God. It reminds me that God has made himself known to me and available to me, and here is my moment to appreciate this wonderful gift. This gift is available to all but requires that we be aware and seek it.

* * * * *

Keep Me Free

Blessed are You, Lord our God, King of the universe, who has not made me a slave.

The meaning here is largely self-evident, as there is little else more valuable than having the freedom to pursue one's life journey, which is the opposite of being a slave. For me, I take it one step further to express my appreciation to God for having given me open-mindedness, which is a legacy to my parents who were both seekers. Slavery or imprisonment can take both physical and mental forms, and as I recite this particular prayer, I have in my heart a deep appreciation for not suffering either form. I am also reinforced by this prayer to move forward in my day ahead with a commitment to preserving my freedom, and especially my open-mindedness, striving to encounter new people with new ideas that will facilitate personal growth.

* * * * *

Allow Me to Appreciate Me As I Am

Blessed are You, Lord our God, King of the universe, who has not made me a woman. (Women recite: Blessed are You, King of the universe, who has made me in His image.)

In modern times, as all but the most traditional Judaism has been influenced by modern thinking and the women's rights movement for equality, this prayer has been replaced by the one recited in traditional synagogues by women. After careful consideration, I've chosen to stick with the original prayer. I do this because I see that it reflects man's appreciation for woman and not any sense of seeing women as being inferior, which is what detractors believe it to be communicating.

For me, the path that God has established for women is certainly harder than that for men and when I recite this prayer I do so with two thoughts in mind. First, and most literally, I thank God for sparing me the more challenging life journey that awaits women. Also, I say this with a deep appreciation for the instrumental women in my life, without whose strength and commitment to me and family I'd not have the life journey that I enjoy.

Finally, it seems fitting that women say the prayer they do, focusing on how they've been created in God's image. Of course, we all have been created in His image, however, only women share with God the power to create human life. As such, their claim to this closeness is superior.

* * * * *

Thanks for Awakening Me

Blessed are You, Lord our God, King of the universe, who removes sleep from my eyes and slumber from my eyelids.

This is the final prayer of this prayer series. It reinforces that through my relationship with God and my appreciation for his role in creating the world and all life I have the prospect of being truly awakened from my slumber to engage with the world in a heightened state of awareness.

6.

Guide Me Towards the Right Path

And may it be Your will, Lord our God and God of our fathers, to accustom us to Your Torah, and to make us cleave to Your commandments. Do not bring us into sin, nor into transgression or iniquity, nor into temptation or scorn; and may the evil inclination not have mastery over us. Keep us far from an evil person and an evil companion. Make us cleave to the good inclination and good deeds; and compel our inclination to be subservient to You. Grant us this day and every day grace, kindness, and mercy in Your eyes and in the eyes of all who behold us; and bestow bountiful kindness upon us. Blessed are You Lord, who bestows bountiful kindness upon His people Israel.

Temptation is all around us at all times, ready to lure us away from the right and true path. This is part of God's intelligent design. Life is a test and without the temptation to go the wrong way, the test is of no value whatsoever. This prayer recognizes that each of us is capable of falling prey to that temptation and to give in to our own inherent evil inclinations, or to be lured by others around us who have succumbed to temptation and are now themselves on the wrong path.

The point of asking God to keep me on the right path in this prayer is not really that I hope to have God literally watch over me that day. I would imagine that he's a bit too busy to be there with all of us. Instead, I see this prayer as one whose recitation aims to reinforce my own awareness as I prepare to walk out into the world in the morning, knowing that there are many tests that await me, and many temptations to lure me away from my good inclination.

In closing, I ask to be bathed in kindness from God and from all with whom I come in contact, knowing that kindness is contagious and that it will support me in my effort to bring my kindness to the world that day.

ז.

Protect Me
from Evil

May it be Your will, Lord my God and God of
my fathers, to protect me this day and every day
from insolent men and from impudence; from a
wicked man, from an evil neighbor and from evil
slander, from false testimony, from men's hate,
from diseases and from misfortune; from the
destructive adversary, from a harsh judgment,
from an implacable opponent, whether or not
he is a member of the Covenant, and from the
retribution of Gehinom.

This prayer is similar, and maybe a partner to the one immediately preceding it. However, unlike its partner which includes a call to be inclined towards the good, this one focuses solely on avoiding evil. Most of us are decent, well-intentioned people. As a result, it is hard for us to understand evil, or to even believe that it exists. But it does exist and if we open our eyes, we see it manifested daily in the world. And, if we study history, we can see how evil people and evil movements can deceive, seduce, and co-opt decent people. The truth is that we are all very vulnerable to being dragged into evil. This prayer is an acknowledgment of my personal vulnerability in that regard and by stating it every morning and gaining awareness of the risks that await me in my day, I can best safeguard myself. Again, I am not really praying to God to keep me from evil (although it would be lovely if he did), but instead, guessing that he's a bit too busy to watch my every move that day, I am making a morning proclamation that creates personal awareness so that I keep my eyes open and remain alert with the hope that alertness will remain with me throughout the day, providing me with my true north.

The last word of this prayer may not be familiar to most of you, but it is a place on the outskirts of Jerusalem. It is a valley, called the Valley of Hinnom (With "Ge" meaning "of"), where long ago children were burned as sacrifices to the Ammonite god Moloch. In the Gospels, authors describe Jesus as using this word to describe the opposite of life in the Kingdom. I suppose it can be thought of like a hell.

8.

Thank You for the Roadmap of Your Teachings

Blessed are You, Lord our God, King of the universe, who has sanctified us with His commandments, and commanded us concerning the words of the Torah. And make the teachings of Your Torah, Lord our God, pleasant in our mouth and in the mouth of Your entire people, the House of Israel, and may we and our children and the children of Your entire people, the House of Israel, all be knowers of Your Name and the students of Your Torah for its own sake. Blessed are You Lord, who teaches the Torah to His people Israel.

This prayer is a part of my daily acknowledgment that God has taken an active role in my life and in the world itself. I remind myself that God has created a purposeful life for me and that everything in this world was created in a form of harmony for all people to live a life from which they can all derive some benefits and value from.

To ensure that we humans can derive maximum value from our lives, God has given us laws that, if adhered to, will allow us to accomplish this goal both for ourselves and to help facilitate that for others too. These laws of God are not limitations or punishments, nor are they laws to benefit one group of people and to keep down another, but instead they are guidelines to a better life of purpose and greater fulfillment for us all.

In the second part of this prayer, I pray for my fellow men and women that they also gain an understanding through the study of God's laws and through prayer of the value of these laws in their lives. I acknowledge that I am not here alone and in fact am completely interdependent with all others in the world. If I am aware of and adhere to God's laws but the majority of others do not, then my life journey will surely not be as pleasant, nor will I experience my full potential benefit. In reciting this portion, I realize that I have a responsibility to myself, to God, and to my fellow men and women, to spread God's teachings and laws and their value to as many as I can, both by deed and by word.

9.

Thank You for the Burden of Your Trust

Blessed are You, Lord our God, King of the universe, who has chosen us from among all nations and given us His Torah. Blessed are You Lord, who gives the Torah.

When I recite this prayer, I feel a sense of being a part of history and of having inherited both a legacy as well as a responsibility. As I wrote in my explanation of the immediately preceding prayer, once people understand that God's laws are essential to a decent world wherein all can experience their full potential and that buy-in from others is critical, it becomes incumbent on those people to both live in accordance with those laws as well as to share their insights with others. Thus, when I recite this prayer, along with a few others too, I understand the burden that comes with being "chosen" to have received the Torah, or God's teachings.

This notion of being chosen has naturally led to enmity from others towards Jews. I believe that this is misguided on a number of important counts. First, as I explained, being chosen is a burden as much as it is a gift. Jews who accept having been chosen by God are burdened to both learn God's laws and to live in accordance with them. While this is a rewarding path to be sure, it involves making sacrifices. Second, the Torah and God's teachings exist and there is nothing to prevent them being studied and embraced by anyone. In fact, in the Jewish teachings, a convert to Judaism, or a person not born to Jewish parents but who makes a choice to live according to Jewish laws and traditions, is to be admired as being more of a Jew than those born to Jews. These teachings explain that one born a Jew had no choice in the matter, while a convert has actively made a choice to embrace the Torah.

10.

The Ancient Priestly Blessing

And the Lord spoke to Moses, saying: Speak to Aaron and to his sons, saying, "Thus shall you bless the children of Israel; say to them: 'The Lord bless you and guard you. The Lord makes his countenance to shine upon you and be gracious to you. The Lord turns His countenance toward you and grants you peace.

And they shall set My name upon the children of Israel, and I shall bless them."

When I recite this prayer, I recall my father placing his hands on my head when I was young and saying this very same blessing for me each Friday evening when we were together to welcome the Sabbath. Since becoming a father, I have upheld that very same tradition, conveying this "priestly blessing" upon each of my children.

When I was last in Israel with my wife, we walked from our hotel and passed by the Canadian embassy in Jerusalem. There was a small archaeological dig site just adjacent to the embassy which revealed a wall buried below today's ground level, and on that wall in Hebrew was this very same priestly blessing that God passed on to Moses, to be given to his brother Aaron and Aaron's sons, who were the high priests, to bestow upon the people Israel. It was so moving for me to see that this prayer that my father bestowed upon me long ago, and that I have carried forward to my children, went back more than two thousand years as was evidenced at this site in Jerusalem. It was a reminder that I am part of a family of people who have been praying to God and using similar wording for so long.

11.

The Guidelines to Being a Good Person

These are the precepts for which no fixed measure is prescribed: leaving crops on the edge of the field for the poor, the gift of the first fruits, the pilgrimage offerings brought when appearing before the Lord on the Three Festivals, deeds of kindness, and the study of the Torah.

These are the precepts, the fruits of which man enjoys in this world, while the principal reward remains in the world to come: honoring one's father and mother, performing deeds of kindness, early attendance in the house of prayer morning and evening, hospitality to strangers, visiting the sick, dowering the bride, escorting the dead, concentration in prayer, bringing peace between man and his fellow man and between husband and wife. And the study of Torah is the equivalent to them all.

As I came to study and recite this prayer daily, it dawned on me that most Jews have no real idea of being Jewish and of living a Jewish life. I have probably known many hundreds of Jews in my life, and if asked what it is that makes them Jewish they'd mostly answer that their mother was Jewish or that they were circumcised. They would have nothing to say about actions they take in their daily lives that they would identify with as being influenced by or informed by their being Jewish. Until I familiarized myself with this prayer, I maybe was in the same situation. With this prayer, I remind myself what it is that makes me a Jew, and what the daily burdens and responsibilities that come with being Jewish are. In essence, this prayer lays out the steps that I need to take in my life to make me a good human being. I know that if I can adhere to the precepts listed in this prayer, that I will have lived a good day and will have been a good person who made a positive contribution to the world. I am reminded daily that these are specific action steps that I need to take in my daily life journey to reinforce my commitment to living a purposeful and even righteous life.

Many of these actions (charity, visiting the sick, etc.) involve performing good deeds, or just being a good and helpful person. Then there is the emphasis on the study of the Torah, which is God's word, and I suppose that if one invests of themselves to become close to these teachings then by definition, they'll choose the right path. The part of this prayer that stands out for me especially is the obligation of honoring of parents and the emphasis of its import, coming as the first of the ten items listed in that second paragraph. Not coincidentally, this mandate is also very prominently positioned in the Ten Commandments, on the first tablet along with the four commandments involving man's responsibilities to God. I believe that we can honor our parents throughout every day when we act in a manner that would make them proud of us, and thus adhering to this mandate is a path to righteousness. Though my parents have passed long ago, they and their parents are always paramount in my mind, and my desire to honor them and to make them proud of me is what surely keeps me on the right path in my life.

12.

The Golden Rule

I hereby receive the active commandment of loving others as myself.

This statement is akin to the Golden Rule that we're all familiar with—"Do onto others as you would have done to you." I believe that by adding in the concept of love, the meaning is amped up to a much more intense level. To love others is clearly a higher order of commitment than to simply do unto them as you'd have done to you.

It is with the daily uttering of these words that I re-commit to bringing my very best to the lives of others. There is no doubt in my mind that this mindset accrues significant benefits to me on so many levels. Most obviously, my life has been deeply enriched by the many wonderful friendships that have resulted

51

from my having this mentality. I also suspect that the strength and physical well-being that I've been blessed with is also tied somehow to my daily pursuit of this attitude of abundance.

13.

Thanks for Always Being There With Me

How precious is your kindness, O God! How goodly are your tents, O Jacob, your dwelling places, O Israel! And I, through Your abundant kindness, come into Your house; I bow toward Your holy sanctuary in awe of You. May my prayer to You, Lord, be at a propitious time; God, in Your abounding kindness, answer me with Your true deliverance.

This prayer begins with the brief statement or affirmation that acknowledges that God's relationship with me and with all humanity is founded on His kindness and benevolence. It affirms that all that befalls me in my life, and my life itself is a gift and is intended to facilitate my personal learning and growth. With this in mind, I bring a level of positivism to my day that I know will enhance my ability to be productive.

I say the second paragraph as a natural extension of the first, as it reinforces my acknowledgment and appreciation for God's presence in my life, an actual constant and physical presence. It is an affirmation that I am always in God's sanctuary, which while I prefer it being in nature rather than inside of a building, can literally be anywhere on earth inasmuch as everything is a part of God's world.

14.

The Lord is With Me, I Shall Not Fear

Lord of the universe, who reigned before anything was created—at the time when by His will all things were made, then was His name proclaimed King. And after all things shall cease to be, the Awesome One will reign alone. He was, He is, and He shall be in glory. He is one, and there is no other to compare to Him, to consort with Him. Without beginning, without end, power and dominion belong to Him. He is my God and my ever-living Redeemer, the strength of my lot in time of distress. He is my banner and my refuge, my portion on the day I call. Into his hand I entrust my spirit, when I sleep and when I wake. And with my soul, my body too, the Lord is with me, I shall not fear.

There are a few prayers that really stand out for me, and this is one of them. The main reason for its importance to me is captured in the final sentence, whereby I establish that I will live my day ahead without any fear.

In my mind, fear is the enemy of a joyful, fulfilling, and meaningful life. Fear is natural for humans, and it is so easy to understand the paralyzing effect of living in fear. We have no clue how or why we got to this life, there is no rule book to guide us while we're here, and we know that death and pain, disappointment, and suffering awaits us. With those realities affecting our state of mind consciously or subconsciously it is quite amazing that anyone can stumble their way into finding any peace or happiness.

With this prayer, and especially with the capstone final proclamation, I acknowledge that I am here because of God, who is all-powerful and all-good, and with that knowledge I can move forward in my day without any fear. I know that whatever happens that day, whatever pain or disappointment that I may experience, it is part of God's divine plan and thus is intended to be for my benefit. There is nothing more powerful or more important than living a life without fear, and this prayer is key in reminding me of that every day.

15.

Loving God is the Precursor to Loving Everything or Anything

Hear, O Israel, the Lord is our God, the Lord is One. Blessed be the name of His glorious kingdom forever and ever.

You shall love the Lord your God with all your heart, with all your soul, and with all your might. And these words which I command you today shall be upon your heart. You shall teach them thoroughly to your children, and you shall speak of them when you sit in your house and when you walk on the road, when you lie down and when you rise. You shall bind them as a sign upon your hand, and they shall be for a reminder between your eyes. And you shall write them upon the doorposts of your house and upon your gates.

And it will be, if you will diligently obey My commandments which I enjoin upon you this day, to love the Lord your God and to serve Him with all your heart and with all your soul, I will give rain for your land at the proper time, the early rain and the late rain, and you will gather in your grain, your wine, and your oil. And I will give grass for your fields for your cattle, and you will eat and be sated. Take care lest your heart be lured away, and you turn astray and worship alien gods and bow down to them for then the Lord's wrath will flare up against you, and He will close the heavens so that there will be no rain and the earth will not yield its produce, and you will swiftly perish from the good land which the Lord gives you. Therefore, place these words of Mine upon your heart and upon your soul, and bind them for a sign on your hand, and they shall be for a reminder between your eyes. You shall teach them to your children, to speak of them when you sit in your house and when you walk on the road, when you lie down and when you rise. And you shall inscribe them on the doorposts of your house and on your gates—so that your days and the days of your children may be prolonged on the land which the Lord swore to your fathers to give to them for as long as the heavens are above the earth.

The Lord spoke to Moses, saying: Speak to the children of Israel and tell them to make for themselves fringes on the corners of their garments throughout their generations, and to attach a thread of blue on the fringe of each corner. They shall be to you as tzitzit, and you shall look upon them and remember all the commandments of the Lord and fulfill them, and you will not follow after your heart and after your eyes by which you go astray—so that you may remember and fulfill all My commandments and be holy to your God. I am the Lord your God who brought you out of the land of Egypt to be your God; I, the Lord, am your God.

This prayer, called the "Sh'ma" for its first Hebrew word meaning "listen," or "hear," is unquestionably the central prayer of the Jewish people. It has one primary message, which is reiterated throughout the first two-thirds of the prayer, and simply states the imperative that we love God with our full passion. When I said this prayer as a young man, I mistakenly assumed that inasmuch as I was praying to God, that it was God who craved my love. Then, as I gained a better understanding of the whole purpose of prayer and realized that I was praying only to improve myself and for my benefit, that I began to see this prayer's true value and purpose.

I realize that a godless life is one that naturally leads to a fractured everyman-for-himself society, informed by deep fear and insecurity, that decays and degenerates into a hell. Conversely, a life that is informed by an appreciation for God and His role in the world, naturally leads to extreme love and deep appreciation for God, which in turn leads to a life of fulfillment, of peace, and of kindness to others and to all of God's creations.

The second section of this prayer eerily predicts that the absence of a love for God will lead to environmental disaster and a shortened life for us and our offspring on this earth. Of course it makes perfect sense. A love for God and an appreciation for the blessings He has bestowed upon us, including the earth's intricate systems, would naturally lead us all to treat these systems with great reverence. Conversely, the absence of love for God, and a lack of appreciation for His blessings, would naturally lead to the debasement of our earth and all of its systems. That we have seen a horrible debasement of all of earth's systems in recent times can, in my mind, be directly linked to the diminished role that religion plays in the lives of most.

The final section of this prayer speaks to the fringes that very observant Jews wear daily as an undergarment, and that most Jewish men wear as a prayer shawl when they pray. Like the skullcaps, which are interchangeably called "kippot" or "yarmulke's," these fringes, called "tzitzit," serve as reminders of our connection to God and to the influence of the divine in our lives. These twin reminders—the kippot and tzizit—are intended to be acknowledgments that humans, without a God-consciousness, naturally have instincts that incline us to go the wrong way—to act selfishly, or harmfully towards ourselves or others. Interestingly, the requirement to wear these twin reminders is only incumbent upon men, and not women. I believe that this is due to the heightened inclination that men have, as hunters, to act poorly, and women's naturally more nurturing and less aggressive nature.

16.

Prayer Sequence

There are a few prayers that are grouped and follow a theme. This next prayer is called interchangeably the "Amida," which means "Standing," or "Standing Prayer," because it is recited while standing, or the "Sh'mona Esrai," which means eighteen, because it was originally comprised of that many prayers, but now contains nineteen plus a concluding meditation. Along with the Sh'ma, this is one of the two central prayers of Jewish prayer and is to be recited thrice daily.

* * * * *

God's Always Been There

My lord, open my lips and my mouth shall declare Your praise. Blessed are You, Lord our God and God of our fathers, God of Abraham, God of Isaac, and God of Jacob, the great, mighty, and awesome God, exalted God, who bestows bountiful kindness, who creates all things, who remembers the piety of the Patriarchs, and who, in love, brings a redeemer to their children's children, for the sake of His name. O' King, You are a helper, a savior, and a shield. Blessed are You, Lord, Shield of Abraham.

The Amidah opens with a powerful reminder of God's connection with me and all those reciting this prayer. He was the father of the great patriarchs, our ancestors from thousands of years ago. It is a reminder of his permanence and man's impermanence. All of those great men are long gone, but God is still there for us and will be there for our great grandchildren too. This opening proclamation also reminds us of God's inherent goodness and love, and interestingly reminds us that God will one day bring us a redeemer, a Messiah. I imagine that my Christian friends will find this concept to be quite familiar. In the end, the prayer emphasizes God's connection to Abraham. Abraham was the first Jew, inasmuch as it was he who was the first monotheist. It was he who first sought and established a personal relationship with God. And it was he who first displayed real love and faith for God.

* * * * *

God Constantly Breathes Life Into Us

You are mighty forever, my Lord, You resurrect the dead; You are powerful to save. He causes the dew to descend (said in spring/summer)/He causes the wind to blow and the rain to fall (said in fall/winter).

He sustains the living with loving kindness, resurrects the dead with great mercy, supports the falling, heals the sick, releases the bound, and fulfills His trust to those who sleep in the dust. Who is like you, mighty One! And who can be compared to You, who brings death and restores life, and causes deliverance to spring forth!

You are trustworthy to revive the dead. Blessed are You Lord, who revives the dead.

Here, we again affirm God's kindness and love for his people. Yet, the most noteworthy and perplexing element of this prayer for me, is the reference to God reviving or resurrecting the dead. In my youth, I had a silly notion that this prayer was a ghoulish, Halloween-like relic from a past when people believed in the physical revival of dead bodies. And then, one day it hit me that this prayer was referring to our consciousness or our soul, and not our bodies. I realized that daily life without a God-consciousness is one in which people are preoccupied with survival, and thus each day is dominated by a competition for resources. In such a world, our worst inclinations and actions are destined to be dominant. And in such a world our souls, or our highest form of life, are deadened. It is only through our connection to God, which connection is reinforced through daily prayer, that we are revived, that we come to life fully. This prayer describes that beautifully.

* * * * *

God Made Me, So I'm Special

You are holy and Your Name is holy, and holy beings praise You daily for all eternity. Blessed are You Lord, the holy God.

This short prayer serves to remind me that I was created by God, the holiest of holies, and therefore I too am holy. All of us know our limitations and our frailties. At the root, in spite of whatever act we may put on for the world, it is natural that we feel small, insignificant, and even helpless as we contemplate our mortality as well as our limited ability to make things happen in our lives. This prayer girds me with the strength, the courage, and even the power to bring it hard in the coming day, allowing me to overcome my own fragility and self-doubt with an understanding that I am God's creation and therefore I too have significant strength and capability. I am also inspired by this prayer to try to live up to the "holy" aspect, to make the good choices in my day and not give in to temptations that would undermine my status as a holy creation.

* * * * *

Give Me Wisdom, Ideas, and Clarity Today

You graciously bestow knowledge upon man and teach mortals understanding. Graciously bestow upon us from You, wisdom, understanding and knowledge. Blessed are You Lord, who graciously bestows knowledge.

I have long wondered where ideas emanate from. It is wondrous, right? Where did all the innovative thinking and knowledge that has moved humanity forward come from? I have come to believe that it is in the air, part of some invisible field of energy that is available for us to all tap into, to channel into the world and bring to life in the form of human creativity and achievement.

At some point early in my Wall Street career, I decided to embrace the idea of experiencing life in general and work in particular in an improvisational state. So, when I had meetings I would do no preparation. I'd not want to know the background of the people with whom I was to meet, nor did I want to know their agenda. I believed that if I did that research I would inevitably develop preconceived ideas that would inhibit my ability to really feel their energy and passion, to hear them and really listen to their plans, and to react with authenticity and the inspiration derived from the world's energy field. That approach has served me well in all facets of my life. As a result, I feel so much more alive not knowing exactly what is coming my way nor how I might react, but completely trusting my instincts, my ability to react with authenticity, and believing that God's energy field—imbued with wisdom, knowledge, and understanding—will help me react appropriately and optimally.

* * * * *

I'm Not Perfect. Please Always Forgive Me. I'm Trying

Cause us to return, our Father, to Your Torah; draw us near, our King, to Your service; and bring us back to You in whole-hearted repentance. Blessed are You Lord, who desires penitence.

Pardon us, our Father, for we have sinned; forgive us, our King, for we have transgressed; for You are a good and forgiving God. Blessed are You Lord, gracious One who pardons abundantly.

O behold our affliction and wage our battle; redeem us speedily for the sake of Your Name, for You God are the mighty redeemer. Blessed are You Lord, Redeemer of Israel.

In this series of prayers, we ask God for forgiveness for our many transgressions, and we acknowledge that God wishes for us to be more repentant in our daily lives. We all mess up, and frequently. And yet, it is rare for people to acknowledge their mistakes and still rarer to apologize and ask for forgiveness. The process of apologizing, or repenting, has so much value. First, it begins the healing process with those we may have aggrieved. Second, and equally important, by acknowledging our misdeeds and our inherent inclination towards waywardness, we instill in ourselves a sense of humility that I believe leads us to becoming better people. Finally, by acknowledging what we did wrong we plant a seed in our consciousness that hopefully will enable us to not make that same mistake again.

* * * * *

Heal Us

Heal us, O Lord, and we will be healed; help us and we will be saved; for You are our praise. Grant complete cure and healing to all our wounds; for You, Almighty King, are a faithful and merciful healer. Blessed are You Lord, who heals the sick of His people Israel.

When reciting this prayer, I keep in mind those close to me who need healing, me included. I consciously try with my prayer to direct God's healing energy that he has infused into the world towards these individuals in my life who need that to help them overcome physical or emotional suffering.

* * * * *

Bless This Year

Bless for us, Lord our God, this year and all the varieties of its produce for good; and bestow blessing (said during the spring and summer season)/dew and rain for blessing (said in the fall and winter season) upon the face of the earth. Satisfy us from Your bounty and bless our year like other good years, for blessing; for You are a generous God who bestows goodness and blesses the years. Blessed are You Lord, who blesses years.

In this prayer, I aim to once again call to the energy that God has created and direct it through prayer to ensure that this year is among the "good" ones. For me it is a pretty straightforward prayer and I say it with my full commitment.

* * * * *

Bring Us Together

Sound the great shofar (ancient horn) for our freedom; raise a banner to gather our exiles and bring us together from the four corners of the earth into our land. Blessed are You Lord, who gathers the dispersed of His people Israel.

This prayer is a call to God to bring the people of Israel together into the land of Israel, their homeland. Since the destruction of the second great Jewish temple in Jerusalem by the Romans in 70 CE, the Jewish people have lived mostly in diaspora, as minorities in foreign lands, often persecuted. In 1948, in the wake of the Holocaust when Jews were truly threatened with extinction, modern Israel was again established and recognized as the Jewish homeland. Of course, since then, Israel has been besieged by constant hostilities, which is recurring in a terrible way as of this writing. Implicit in this prayer is the hope that the Jewish people can one day live in their homeland in total peace.

I also find something else fascinating in this prayer, which seems to call for God's help in herding all Jews to reside together in Israel. In my mind, we live in God's world, which means that everything is perfect, purposeful, and exactly as it should be— even the things we find to be distasteful and worse. So, antisemitism, which I prefer to call "Jew-hatred," and which has been a constant in the world and even in places with no Jews, must also be part of God's plan and purposeful. To me, this prayer helps explain in part the purpose of Jew-hatred. If it did not exist, and at times become so unpalatable as to cause Jews to want or need to flee their diaspora homelands, then this prayer could never be fulfilled. You see, it could be that the inspiration for the fulfillment of this prayer is the presence of Jew-hatred.

* * * * *

Bless Us With Your Leadership

Restore our judges as in former times, and our counselors as of yore; remove from us sorrow and sighing, and reign over us, You alone, O Lord, with kindness and compassion, with righteousness and justice. Blessed are You Lord, King who loves righteousness and justice.

As I recite this prayer, I think about how cursed humanity seems to be with regard to its leadership, and I pray earnestly for the day when God himself, or others who meet his criteria of kindness, compassion, righteousness, and justice lead us. I believe that to lead one must be truly religious, aware of God and thus appropriately humble and thus not easily corruptible.

* * * * *

Punish the Wicked

Let there be no hope for informers and may all heretics and all the wicked instantly perish; may all the enemies of Your people be speedily extirpated; and may You swiftly uproot, break, crush and subdue the reign of wickedness speedily in our days. Blessed are You Lord, who crushes enemies and subdues the wicked.

I believe that we are on this earth to find ourselves, to navigate the world, to explore, to try things then once we get feedback to recalibrate, always seeking to learn and improve. People who get in the way of this process, who inhibit our freedoms and thus undermine the potential of our journey represent an anti-life force. This prayer is one in which we ask God to eliminate those people from our journey so that we may pursue our destinies of optimal growth.

* * * * *

Stand With the Righteous, Always

May Your mercies be aroused, Lord our God, upon the righteous, upon the pious, upon the elders of Your people, the House of Israel, upon the remnant of their sages, upon the righteous proselytes and upon us. Grant ample reward to all who truly trust in Your Name and place our lot among them; may we never be disgraced, for we have put our trust in You. Blessed are You Lord, the support and security of the righteous.

There is an interesting juxtaposition of this prayer to God to reward and protect the righteous and faithful following immediately the prayer to punish the wicked, which occupies a part of my focus when I recite this prayer. I clearly wish to be counted at least among the faithful, if not the righteous or pious too, and surely not be counted among the wicked.

This prayer also reminds me to act towards others in my day as I wish God to act towards me and humanity. We all have those who have placed their faith and trust in us, including our families, our employees, partners, and co-workers, those who have invested in us, including our parents and ancestors. I must walk the walk as pertains to my responsibilities to always care for them, to be mindful of the trust they've invested in me and the responsibilities that come naturally from that trust.

* * * * *

Bond Us to Our Land
and Our Heritage

Return in mercy to Jerusalem Your city and dwell therein as You have promised; speedily establish therein the throne of David Your servant and rebuild it soon in our days as an everlasting edifice. Blessed are You Lord, who rebuilds Jerusalem.

I srael is central to Judaism, and Jerusalem its capital is central to and representative of Israel in this prayer. There is something magical about Israel, and especially about Jerusalem—a special energy that is palpable when you're there. For lack of any better word, it feels holy. While saying this prayer I am reminded of the importance of Israel and Jerusalem to the Jewish people and to me personally. It feels to me like a sort of a proclamation that deepens my emotional ties with Jerusalem. I recall in my youth beginning every school day with a recital of America's Pledge of Allegiance, which to me had the same effect of bonding me deeply with the U.S.

* * * * *

Bring Our World Salvation

Speedily cause the scion of David Your servant to flourish, and increase his power by Your salvation, for we hope for Your salvation all day. Blessed are You Lord, who causes the power of salvation to flourish.

This is a prayer for the Messiah, who is promised to be a direct descendant of King David, to come and deliver us to a better place than we find ourselves in here on earth. I must admit to having some mixed feelings about this prayer, and even the notion of salvation. I deeply believe that God created this world and all of us with intelligent design and purpose, so it seems awkward to be begging God (all day, as the prayer says) to save us from this life of purpose that He designed. So, I recite it with humility, knowing that there are many things that are far beyond my capability to ever understand. I accept that praying for salvation and for a Messiah, and indeed the whole idea of a Messiah, is one of those things, and I recite this prayer while simultaneously hoping that God may one day open my eyes and illuminate me a bit more as to what this is truly all about.

* * * * *

Hear Our Prayers

Here our voice, Lord our God; merciful Father, have compassion upon us and accept our prayers in mercy and favor, for You are God who hears prayers and supplications; do not turn us away empty-handed from You, or King, for You hear the prayer of everyone. Blessed are You Lord, who hears prayer.

Look with favor, Lord our God, on Your people Israel and pay heed to their prayer; restore the service to Your Sanctuary and accept with love and favor Israel's fire-offerings and prayer; and may the service of Your people Israel always find favor. May our eyes behold Your return to Zion in mercy. Blessed are You Lord, who restores His Divine Presence to Zion.

These two prayers both ask God to hear our prayers and to receive them with favor. The second of them also is a plea to restore the sacred temple in Jerusalem, where Jews historically communicated with God through prayer and sacrificial offerings. To me, these prayers reinforce that there is a channel open for each of us to communicate with God, and that He is there for us to turn to in communication.

* * * * *

Your Daily Miracles
Are Wondrous

We thankfully acknowledge that You are the Lord our God and God of our fathers forever. You are the strength of life, the shield of our salvation in every generation. We will give thanks to You and recount Your praise evening, morning, and noon, for our lives which are committed into Your hand, for our souls which are entrusted to You, for Your miracles which are with us daily, and for Your continual wonders and beneficences. You are the Beneficent One, for Your mercies never cease; the Merciful One, for Your kindnesses never end; for we always place our hope in You.

And for all these, may Your Name, our King, be continually blessed, exalted and extolled forever and all time. And all living things shall forever thank You and praise Your great Name eternally, for You are good. God, You are our everlasting salvation and help, O benevolent God. Blessed are You Lord, Beneficent is Your Name, and to You it is fitting to offer thanks.

I take these two companion prayers as a call to remind myself throughout the day ahead of the wonders and miracles that I encounter and to keep in my heart a deep sense of appreciation to God for all of them. I also focus on the call for me to "recount" these wonders and miracles in my daily dialogue, both to reinforce awareness of God's influence on all of earth for myself as well as to help create awareness, and all the benefits that come therefrom, for others and especially for my children.

* * * * *

Bestow Peace

Bestow peace, goodness and blessing, life, graciousness, kindness and mercy upon us and upon all Your people Israel. Bless us, our Father, all of us as one, with the light of Your countenance. For by the light of Your countenance You gave us, Lord our God, the Torah of life and a love for righteousness, charity, blessing, mercy, life, and peace. May it be favorable in Your eyes to bless Your people Israel at all times and at every moment with Your peace. Blessed are You Lord who blesses His people Israel with peace.

There are two important messages for me in this prayer. Primary here is the focus on peace, the pleading with God for peace, and the showing of appreciation to God for whatever peace we might enjoy in this world that is not typically too peaceful. The second important element that I find in this prayer is the thanking of God for imbuing me and my fellow Jews, through his gift of the teachings of His Torah, with an innate love for "righteousness, charity, blessing, mercy, life, and peace." This speaks directly to the very essence of the religion that I adore and that I attempt to practice and embody throughout my life on a daily basis. I am certain that a love for these principals, and their embodiment in one's life will lead to a life well lived.

* * * * *

Guard My Tongue
and My Temper

May the words of my mouth and the meditation of my heart be acceptable before You, Lord, my Strength and my Redeemer.

My God, guard my tongue from evil and my lips from speaking deceitfully. Let my soul be silent to those who curse me; let my soul be as dust to all. Open my heart to Your Torah and let my soul eagerly pursue Your commandments. As for all those who plot evil against me, hasten to annul their counsel and frustrate their design. Let them be as chaff before the wind; let the angel of the Lord thrust them away. That Your beloved ones may be delivered, help with Your right hand and answer me. Do it for the sake of Your Name; do it for the sake of Your right hand; do it for the sake of Your Torah; do it for the sake of Your holiness. May the words of my mouth and the meditation of my heart be acceptable before You, Lord, my Strength and my Redeemer.

He who makes peace in His heavens, may He make peace for us and for all Israel; and say, Amen.

This is the concluding prayer of this prayer group called the Amidah and there are a few things in it that really touch me and influence me in my daily life. First, is the recognition that we are all so very prone to gossip and dishonesty that we must actually pray to God to strengthen us and guard us against that inclination, and that these are both things that one must strive desperately to avoid.

I also find the approach to dealing with those who may have bad intentions towards us extremely fascinating. In this prayer, we simultaneously ask God to frustrate their efforts while also asking God to give us tranquility in the face of evil and betrayal, to not have us seek revenge but instead to have us be silent and entrust God to handle our business.

That the prayer finishes with another emphasis on peace would be consistent with this inasmuch as it underscores that the pursuit of revenge will lead to a cycle of hostilities—the opposite of peace. So, in reality, this prayer is essentially another one for peace.

‏יז.‏

A Reminder of the Importance of Prayer

May it be Your will, Lord our God and God of our fathers, that the Holy Temple be speedily rebuilt in our days and grant us our portion in Your Torah.

This brief prayer reinforces our hope in a full return of the Jewish people to their home in Israel, as symbolized by the rebuilding of the Holy Temple, which was last destroyed by the Romans more than 2,000 years ago, and which destruction led directly to more than 2,000 years of Jews living in a diaspora, with no homeland. It also reinforces the centrality of prayer to Jewish life, and the importance of prayer to any healthy society, inasmuch as the prayer is not seeking for the return of the homeland itself but instead focused on the rebuilding of the Temple, where prayer is to be conducted.

18.

Clean My Slate Anew and Those of My Loved Ones

Our God, and God of our fathers, may our prayers come before You, and do not turn away from our supplication, for we are not so impudent and obdurate as to declare before You, Lord our God and God of our fathers, that we are righteous and have not sinned. Indeed, we and our fathers have sinned.

We have transgressed, we have acted perfidiously, we have robbed, we have slandered. We have acted perversely and wickedly, we have willfully sinned, we have done violence, we have imputed falsely. We have given evil counsel, we have lied, we have scoffed, we have rebelled, we have provoked, we have been disobedient, we have committed iniquity, we have wantonly transgressed, we have oppressed, we have been obstinate. We have committed evil, we have acted perniciously, we have acted abominably, we have gone astray, we have led others astray.

We have strayed from Your good precepts and ordinances, and it has not profited us. Indeed, You are just in all that has come upon us, for You have acted truthfully, and it is we who have acted wickedly.

God, You are slow to anger. You are called the All-Merciful One, and You have taught the way of repentance. Remember this day and every day the greatness of your compassion and loving kindness toward the descendants of Your beloved. Turn to us in mercy, for You are the All-Merciful One. With supplication and prayer we approach You, as You have made known to Moses the humble one in days gone by. Turn from Your fierce anger, as it is written in Your Torah. May we find shelter and lodge in the shadow of Your wings, as on the day when "the Lord descended in a cloud." Overlook our transgression and erase our trespass, as on the day when "He stood with him (Moses) there." Heed our plea and hearken to our supplication, as on the day when "he (Moses) invoked the Name of the Lord;" and there it is said:

And the Lord passed before him and proclaimed: "Lord, Lord, benevolent God, compassionate and gracious, slow to anger and abounding in kindness and truth; He preserves kindness for two thousand generations, forgiving iniquity, transgression and sin, and He cleanses."

Merciful and gracious One, we have sinned before You; have mercy upon us and save us.

In this final prayer, I appeal to God to forgive me for all that I must be forgiven for, and I ask God to do likewise for every member of my family. The focus of this prayer for me is the penultimate paragraph beginning with "Lord, Lord..." in which I beseech God to wipe the slate clean for me and my loved ones. I recite this paragraph four separate times, each time focusing my attention differently. First, I recite it with my wife and myself in my consciousness. Next I recite it with each of my five children in my consciousness. Third, I recite it while focusing on those who were very dear to me and who have passed on, including my parents, my four grandparents, my uncle and aunt, a dear friend, and our first family dog Snowy. In this version I pray both for their forgiveness as well as for them to intercede with God on my behalf, knowing that they are closer to Him now than I am. In my final recitation, I concentrate on my brother and his wife Hayley, Maria Garay, who has lived with me for more than 30 years and has taken great care of me and my family, on my 6 siblings-in-law and their families, and on our beautiful family dogs whose souls and capacities for love are so pure.

And with this prayer I complete my morning prayer ritual, am refreshed, and I have a healthy and positive state of mind that will give me the best chance of living that day with maximum joy and productivity.

About the Author
Ethan Penner

In a world where we think of prayer and spiritual practice as being the domain of clergy and religious scholars—professional men and women who earn their pay running a congregation and who study and teach religion—I am not the person you would naturally expect to write a book on prayer and God. I have made my living working as a financier, a Wall Street man, and a professional real estate investor. I began my career path at age 22 after graduating college and went down those paths, gaining mastery and even acclaim. But I was raised by thoughtful parents who were both spiritual seekers, and who (especially mom) taught me to live life in a fully aware state. It has been through the totality of my life journey—my professional life and my personal life, my roles as producer, provider, husband, father, and friend, my experiences, my observations, my successes and my failures—that I learned about life.

In the early 1990's the U.S. real estate industry was on the verge of complete collapse. Fueled by historical declines in value, all lenders withdrew from the market all at once, leaving all those owners of real estate unable to repay their maturing loans. It was in that moment that I, at 31 years old a total outsider to the real estate industry, introduced the industry to the capital markets, built the largest real estate finance company in U.S. history to that date, and provided the industry with a pathway to survival. In this moment of desperation, it fell to an outsider to provide the industry with a better path forward. I learned then that this is natural and logical because insiders are beholden to the same ideas that caused the problems and collapse in the first place. Thus, in today's world where God is not on the radar for too many people, it shouldn't be too great a shock that the path to remedying this might not come from the insiders whose well-meaning efforts have led us to this moment of crisis.

I am not a scholar in the traditional sense. I have not invested the majority of my time learning by reading or researching, but instead by living. I cannot quote from the wise words of too many great people from the past, but I can share the insights that

I gained through living a life that has been very full and whose experiences have been very diverse. It is this life journey that has taught me many different perspectives, allowing me to gain understanding and empathy. Importantly, I have lived my life in a high state of awareness.

My parents were both scholars and spiritual seekers. They were Jewish and not just in the perfunctory sense that most Jews understand but in the deepest sense, whereby their Jewishness informed most all aspects of their lives. I had the great privilege of attending a truly great Jewish parochial elementary school called Westchester Day School, where my parents' teachings were reinforced for me. As I hit my teenage years, I largely abandoned my Jewish practice, but the teachings and values continued to inform how I lived my life.

I was fortunate to have achieved a reasonably high level of financial success before age 40, which, combined with my spiritual upbringing, led me to leave Wall Street and dramatically slow down my work life. In reflection, I realize that it was that decision that has led me to directly to publishing this book as well as my first one, Greatness is a Choice. You see, for most people, the treadmill of life is moving very quickly, leaving no time to ponder life's great questions. In times past, this pondering fell naturally upon clergy, who were supported by community with a mandate to then share their insights and guide their community that were available as a result of having the luxury of having the time to ponder.

My full life journey includes having been raised by divorced parents who didn't get along, living in poor economic conditions as a child and having worked since age nine, being exposed to religious teachings, living a mostly secular life as an adult which included a meteoric and mega-successful career on Wall Street, my own divorce and remarriage, five kids from three different continents, and a lifetime of paying attention and asking questions—of seeking purpose. I have come to believe that purpose is the key to life and have concluded that purpose can only come from a connection to God. My connection begins daily with my prayer ritual, which is rooted in the traditional Jewish prayer book, the very same prayers that Jesus and his apostles would be reciting were they to be alive today. I see that for the world to heal that we all must find our way back to these prayers—Jews and Christians for sure, and perhaps others too. In my friend group I know many people and among those are devout Christians, who are among the finest, most ethical, and most delightful people that I know. Inevitably, whenever I have met these people or their friends the conversation turns to spirituality and I am asked, somewhat awkwardly, what religion I practice. My answer is always the same—I practice the same religion that Jesus did.